"We have an incredible God who has the capability to change our lives far faster than we could ever do on our own."

Kelli Boone

BEYOND LIMITS

How Running from God
Brought Me Closer to God

Kelli Boone

2017

Copyright © 2017
Tribute Publishing, LLC
Frisco, Texas U.S.A.

Beyond Limits
First Edition October 2017

All Worldwide Rights Reserved
ISBN: 9780998286075

All rights reserved. No part of this book may be reproduced, stored in a retrieval system, or transmitted, in any form, or by any means, electronic, mechanical, recorded, photocopied, or otherwise, without the prior written permission of the copyright owner, except by a reviewer who may quote brief passages in a review.

In God We Trust.

Table of Contents

Dedication i

Introduction iii

Chapter 1
My Biggest Deception in Life.......................................1

Chapter 2
What Blocks Your Path? 9

Chapter 3
Do You Remember to Look in the Mirror Every Day?........21

Chapter 4
How Do You Develop Faith from Failure?............................31

Chapter 5
How Running from God, Brought Me Closer to God 39

Chapter 6
Are You Afraid to Go Deeper? 53

Chapter 7
Why Does God Need You to Move? 59

Chapter 8
How Do You Accept God's Forgiveness?............................. 67

Chapter 9
Are You Telling Your Story? 75

Chapter 10
Telling My Story 87

About the Author 99

Dedication

I would like to dedicate this book to God, without him this book would not be possible, my wonderful husband, Jeremy, who encouraged me to pursue my lifelong dream of writing a book, my son, Landon, who is my greatest gift from God and my inspiration, my Mom and Dad, who shaped me into the person I am today, and Pastor Matt Malone, who made me realize that my *beyond limits* story was something that I needed to share with the world.

- Kelli Boone

Introduction

What is a *Beyond Limits* story?

Throughout this book, you will learn strategies that I have used in my own life to uncover my beyond limits story during a time where I felt that I had no purpose. My hopes are that by sharing my story, it will encourage you to find your own story and go beyond any limits that you have ever put on yourself. I would like to start by first defining what a beyond limits story is so that we can move in the same direction together.

A beyond limits story is hidden inside each and every one of us. It's what makes us different, what sets us apart, what drives us, and what gives us a burning desire to go out and change the world in a unique way. It's a story that once uncovered, will give you purpose and a light to the path less traveled. It will make you so excited that nothing will stop you. Everybody has a beyond limits story; it's up to you to find it in your own life and continue moving forward to embrace what God has in store for you. In reading this book, you will learn how to uncover your own story, what holds you back, and how to continue creating a life where you go beyond any limits that you have ever put on yourself. I hope my story encourages you to look deep into your own life to find your own story, to discover your purpose, and create a life of GREATNESS. I'm so excited to go on this journey with you and can't wait to see how it changes your life.

Once you complete this book, I would love for you to share with me and others you're beyond limits story because by sharing your story, you have the power to change the world.

#WhatsYourBeyondLimitsStory?

v

Chapter 1

My Biggest Deception in Life

If you could write a letter offering advice to your younger self, knowing what you know now and what your fears were then, what would you say?

I would tell myself that God has a bigger plan for my life, that he will use my mistakes for good, and that one of the most tragic events in my life would be my greatest blessing and would turn into a ministry that would offer other people hope when life seems hopeless. I would remind myself that the tough times are what will shape me into the person that I am today and to never give up because I will change the world one day!

This is where my story begins.

I was 15 years old and a sophomore in high school. I would love to tell you that I was raised in a Christian home with a solid upbringing and no real issues, but that's not the case. I came from a very broken home with parents who were living with constant doubt, disappointments, and financial struggles.

In not knowing how to deal with this, alcohol became an escape that helped them to forget about their unhappiness and financial struggles and pretend that everything in their lives was great, until the hangover of the next day kicked their lives back into the reality that they never wanted to face in the first place.

Most of my childhood was centered around fighting, unpredictability, and the use of negative words that were said to me, and over time, became who I thought I was as a person. I let those words become a source of hurt, as most of them were directed towards me and the things that I would do wrong. So, I would tell myself those words over and over and began to believe that I was a failure. I let those words define my worth and bring me down like a cowering dog after they have been hit. What I didn't realize at the time was that those words were said from the hearts of my two parents who believed those same things about themselves. They were told similar words from someone that made them believe that they were unworthy. Now, this had trickled into how they parented their kids. Growing up, my parents rarely got along. It was as if they were still finding themselves while they were raising kids at the same time. I would come home from school and have no idea how any night would turn out. Some nights would be calm, while other nights would result in violence, throwing furniture, and holes in the wall.

As you can see, most of my childhood was filled with uncertainty. I was a product of parents who were so focused on their own problems, they were unable to be emotionally available to help me with mine. In a confusing time where I was lost and trying to find myself, I struggled with constant self-doubt. I let the hurtful words that were said to me at home begin to shape me into the failure that I believed myself to be. I then began to think, act, and become that person in real life. Those words were the beginning to the start of my feeling of unworthiness. I did not know this at the time, but this would also be the start to a time of big change down a path that would completely redefine the image I had of myself.

My parents were great at portraying that they had a great life to other people, but behind closed doors there was yelling, hurtful words, and a not so loving marriage. I was raised in a home where I had performance-based acceptance. I was taught that if I made good grades and didn't make mistakes and appeared perfect to the public eye, I was accepted and loved. If I made bad grades or made any mistakes, I was rejected and unworthy. I watched the kids at school that had what I perceived as perfect families and knew that there had to be a better way. I didn't know then what I know now, but at that moment, I made the decision that this would stop with me. I had the choice to become the product of my parents or the solution to my redesigned life, my better life, moving forward. We all have that choice in our lives. It's up to us to decide if we will continue the patterns of our past.

As a child, I was woken up many nights to the sound of yelling so loud that my heart would race and my body would tremble. I remember going to school and hearing kids complain about how their parents made them play sports they didn't want to play or made them get off the phone earlier than they wanted. I remember wishing I had those problems, wishing I had their parents, and longing for that same love and affection that my classmates didn't appreciate. I spent the majority of my elementary school years never talking about the things I experienced at home. I seemed fine from the exterior until something happened that would forever change my life: I got pregnant.

I was 15 years old, barely a teenager, lost, confused, and living proof of my parents' worst fear. The life that seemed so perfect on the surface was now imperfect for everyone to see. The mistakes were now visible and proof to the public and to my parents that I was a failure. In my eyes, this was the biggest mistake that I could have made at this age. How in the world was I going to tell my parents? I began by telling my mom first. As we headed to the doctor to get confirmation of the truth, my mom was, ironically, very supportive. She was strong and refused to let me do what I perceived, at the age of 15, what would be the easy way out and have an abortion. She spoke about how we were going to get through this together and how this was not the end of the world. I remember feeling terrified about what my future would look like and how I would tell my friends at school. I didn't see my mom's vision for my life, but I'm glad that she did, as it was the only bit of courage I had to hang on to during this confusing time in my life. Every time I doubted my capabilities, she was there to pick me up and I'm very grateful for her confident presence in my life at that time.

We sat patiently in the doctor's office letting the silence take over. The doctor walked in and confirmed the truth we already knew; I was pregnant. I was 5 ½ months along. This is when it became very real to me that I could no longer hide from the fear that I didn't want to face. This was my reality. It was time to face it and deal with it head on. What was next? I had to tell my dad.

My mom offered to call and let him know, which I gladly accepted. He wasn't very accepting at first, as he wanted my life to be so much different. He was angry, frustrated, and disappointed. It was as if all the dreams that he wanted me to have to create a much more desirable life than he had growing up, were diminished. Thankfully, he had a long ride home from work to think it over. This allowed his boss the opportunity to share with him the story of his regrets with his own wife having an abortion and how it had a negative effect on their lives. I didn't know it that day, but God was very present in putting the right person in my dad's life to offer him a new perspective and a new light during a seemingly dark situation. Now as if being a freshman in high school wasn't hard enough, I had to tell my friends.

I'm not sure what scared me more, telling my friends or feeling like everyone else would know and judge me. My friends were so curious about everything. It was almost as if my life was a movie and they were interested to see how it played out. I was the only person in my grade who was pregnant. Students that I never talked to would come up to me to ask questions. I felt eyes of shame and judgment come upon me as I walked through the hallways to my locker every day, pretending to be OK, but secretly wanting to disappear on the inside. I wasn't sure who accepted me and who didn't. I wasn't even sure if I accepted myself, as I felt like I was an obvious failure in every way. This was when my biggest deception in my life began.

In an effort to prove to my parents and to the world that I was not a complete failure, I decided to focus on excelling in other areas of my life. I was determined that I would not be a statistic. I would defy the odds. I would show people that, despite my circumstances, I would overcome the odds and succeed. I graduated #10 in my high school graduating class and became the first person in my family to graduate from college. While I should have been proud of these accomplishments, I still felt like it wasn't enough and I couldn't figure out why, until after years of counseling, coaching, and praying, I uncovered a truth I didn't want to face.

I was using my accomplishments to hide from the perceived mistakes that I thought were so bad. Many would think this would be a good coping mechanism, but the underlying issue was that I was achieving what the world perceived to be great things. I was defying the odds. I was doing everything great at the expense of never dealing with the root cause of my problem. I had used the great things I did as a way to cover up the depression and unacceptance I felt from so many people. I had spent the majority of my life feeling like I had to gain the acceptance of others in order for my problem to go away, when in reality, I had to gain the acceptance from myself in order to move forward. This was a hard pill for me to swallow because I had to do one of the hardest things in my life. I had to realize that God had already forgiven me for the things that I had spent years making myself feel guilty for.

My biggest deception in my life was that I was successful. The truth was that I was successful according to the things the world may define as successful. However, I wasn't successfully dealing with myself on the inside. I was letting the pain, fear, and insignificance that I felt become who I was without ever realizing it. I was masking my true problem and letting the celebration of my accomplishments distract me from realizing that I needed to stop and deal with the truth. I honestly didn't want to face it. I didn't think I needed to deal with it. I wanted to pretend that I had it all together. I wanted people to believe that I had it all figured out when I had nothing figured out, except how to feel pain and defeat while never dealing with my true issues. This leads me to ask you a question.

How many of us do this to ourselves? We put off dealing with the things that we know we need to resolve because we are afraid to face reality. We are too prideful to admit that we don't have all the answers. We let our sense of pride prevent us from getting the counseling and help that we truly need in order to get past the battles in our lives and be the best version of ourselves. Other times, we simply aren't aware that we aren't dealing with the real issues that are causing our pain. This was a deception in my life that once I faced, changed my life forever. In the next few chapters of this book, I hope that by sharing my own story of overcoming self-doubt that you will be able to see your story in a way that will help you uncover the thing that is holding you back, face it head on, and use your story to change the world by going beyond any limits you have ever put on yourself.

Chapter 2

What Blocks Your Path?

    I can't do this! I quit! I'm done! I give up! Have you ever said or thought this at some point in your life? We all have. But, what is it that makes some people keep pushing when others stop? The person that keeps persisting has figured out what it is that blocks their path and how to move through it, while the other person who stops is stuck. This chapter will teach you a few questions to ask yourself to discover what it is that holds you back and how to get unstuck from most barriers that keep you from being the best version of yourself every day. But first, I want to start with a story.

Have you ever been in a place in your life where you are on the verge of doing something great but can't quite get there because you don't know what is stopping you from moving forward? This was a constant battle in my life every day. I felt like giving up more times than I could count. As a single parent at a very young age, I had a very low self-image and constantly doubted my worthiness. I knew there were several barriers blocking my path to success, but never knew of a way to uncover those barriers. I was paralyzed by fear and afraid to deal with the truth of what was really holding me back. I always knew in the back of my mind there had to be something better for me. I didn't know how to find it or what to do to get there, but I knew it was out there waiting for me and it was up to me to find it. This is where the first turning point in my life happened.

I was a single parent with a career, working hard to provide for my son, while still trying to find myself. I attended church for the first time in a really long time with some friends who had invited me to a new church they really loved. I had just gotten out of a bad relationship and remember feeling very relieved going to church, as this would be a refreshing way to begin again. I was also extremely nervous. The thoughts of being a teenage mother who wasn't welcome in a previous church so long ago flooded my mind and I began to feel thoughts of shame, unworthiness, and like I didn't belong. We walked in as the music was playing and I remember feeling so out of place as my friends had their hands held high in the air praising God and singing every word to every song that was played. I secretly wanted to disappear. Why did I do this to myself? Church wasn't for single parents. It was for married couples, couples without kids before marriage, and people who were worthy of God's love because their mistakes were easier to cover up than mine. As these thoughts were flooding my mind, I was brought back into the present by a song that caught my attention. The melody flooded my heart and I remember being in awe listening to the words, "Higher than the mountains that I face. Stronger than the power of the grave. Constant through the trial and the change. This one thing remains. Your love never fails. It never gives up. It never runs out on me." It was like God was telling me that no matter what I have done, his love for me has NEVER failed. He still loves me the same. He has forgiven me, even if I haven't forgiven myself. I was brought to tears. After the song ended, and I began wiping away the tears so my friends couldn't see, then we sat down for the message, which was also God's little way of getting through to me.

The pastor's message was about getting rid of the baggage in your life and how allowing that baggage to remain will weigh you down and prevent you from being able to receive God's best in your life. After just getting out of a bad relationship, I knew God was speaking to me that day. He was telling me to move on because he had something way better in store for my life. The church service was exactly what I needed and after that service, I knew that this church was exactly where God had called me to be and I had to go back for more. I had set a goal to start going to church with my friends every Sunday and was so excited to begin this new journey with God.

The following Sunday was approaching and my friends were going out of town so they weren't able to attend church that week. I was super bummed as I was excited to go to church, but fear began to kick in.- Since I didn't know anyone else but them, I didn't go that week, or the following week, or the following, as my friends had reasons why they weren't able to go that I allowed to prevent me from going. After the 4th week, I had decided that enough was enough and I was going back to church with or without my friends. I asked my son, Landon, if he would be interested in coming to church with me, which he agreed. We pulled up to church and I could see that we were going to be a few minutes late and could hear that music had already started inside. The thoughts of shame began to fill my head. I wasn't worthy to be here. Who am I kidding? Why would I do this to myself again? This is going to be so embarrassing. Plus, I'm walking in late and don't know anyone. I walked in feeling shame, guilt, and unworthiness. It was in that moment that my life was forever changed.

The ushers opened the doors and I could clearly hear the words to the song that was playing and was immediately brought to tears as I heard the words, "Your love never fails. It never gives up. It never runs out on me." The only song I knew and desperately needed to hear at that moment. It was God again, telling me that he still loves me no matter what! That nothing is too BIG for him. And that he forgives me. I felt a huge weight lifted off my shoulders and I knew that God knew exactly how to show me that this was where I belonged, even if I doubted it at the time.

What blocked my path was my belief that God had given up on me, that God didn't love me, and that I was not worthy of receiving his grace and forgiveness. God showed me that not only was I worthy of all of that and more, but he wasn't through with me yet. He would use every method he could think of to make sure I heard what he was saying to me loud and clear, even when I doubted. He wasn't giving up on me.

Going to church was the beginning of a massive change in my life. It led me to begin to ask myself these 4 questions that I now ask myself anytime that I feel stuck and am trying to figure out what is holding me back.

1. Am I asking God for help?
2. Am I doing things that are allowing me to move forward?
3. Am I practicing what I preach?
4. Am I getting advice from a biblically sound coach/mentor/pastor?

At this time in my life, I was in constant inner conflict with myself, as my actions did not reflect my words, therefore I was stuck. I didn't practice what I preached, got advice from people who didn't have their own lives together, and I didn't include God in any of the decisions I was making at the time. It was when I began asking myself these questions and answering them honestly that I really started to realize that I needed to make a change.

1. Am I asking God for help?

When I didn't know what to do, I began to ask God for help. I started with a prayer. With very little Bible background and church experience at the time, my prayer sounded something like this, "God, I have no idea what to ask you for, but I need your help. I know I'm not living a life that reflects who you want me to be and I don't know where else to turn. Would you help to show me what you want me to see to begin living the life you want me to live?" This short but simple prayer was something I frequently said to remind myself to involve God in more of the decisions that I needed to make in my everyday life. As my journey into learning more about God progressed, my eyes were opened to a Bible verse that I frequently reflect back on when I am in need of help or just need clarity in my life. Matthew 7:7-8, "Ask and it will be given to you; seek and you will find; knock and the door will be opened to you. For everyone who asks receives; the one who seeks finds; and the one who knocks, the door will be opened." I believe that God is sitting behind the door waiting for us to ask for his help. God wants to help us. He wants to direct us. He wants to open the door for us. So many of us simply don't ask for his help. We walk all the way up to the door and raise our hand with the intention to knock, then let our pride get in the way and stop us from seeing God's best in our lives. We think that we can handle it on our own. We think we are in control and we don't see the value of asking God for his hand in the situations that we face in our lives. Or, we ask one time, don't see instant results, and stop asking. We forget we have to be persistent and sometimes God wants us to experience something in our lives first that will help to lead us to our answer. So, we do nothing and we never give God the opportunity to show us what he can do for us. Here we have an incredible God who has the capability to change our lives far faster than we could ever do on our own, but we don't let him. Instead, we spend years of our lives going in circles, making the same mistakes over and over, and missing out on the opportunities that we don't even realize are in store for us, when all we have to do is ask. This brings me to my next question.

2. Am I doing things that are allowing me to move forward?

I was a fairly new member of our church and fighting with the transition of living a life that represented Jesus and still wanting to live a party lifestyle. I thought that as long as I went to church every Sunday, that it didn't matter how I lived my life the rest of the week. Therefore, I attracted the wrong relationships into my life and found myself in many co-dependent relationships that I knew were bad for me, yet I couldn't figure out why I kept attracting these people and why I felt like I needed to stay in these relationships. In an effort to make a change towards living a better lifestyle, I began to get involved in more activities with my church. That's when I went on a youth retreat as a parent volunteer and met another parent, who I didn't know too well at the time. She told me about her personal struggles in her own life and how she was able to get through them with the help of an amazing biblical counselor. Hearing about her struggles helped me begin to see mine and realize that I may need to look into this path to help me move forward. I ended up getting the name and phone number of this counselor and calling her the following week. I began by taking action on the things that would help me move forward to become who God truly wanted me to become. I knew I needed help and I could no longer embark on this journey to a new life on my own. I had to make that next step. I had to look past my pride and ask someone else for help. This was a great challenge for me personally because I was great at pretending like I had it all together. I didn't want anyone else to see that I really didn't and I always thought counseling was for people with problems worse than mine. What I realized was quite the opposite. Having a biblical counselor helped me grow much deeper in my relationship with God. It helped me love myself again. It helped me become the woman I needed to be to attract the man God wanted for me. It helped me realize that I was living a life with constant inner conflict because I wasn't living a life that represented who God wanted me to be on this Earth. Most importantly, it brought me to begin asking myself this question.

3. Am I practicing what I preach?

Through counseling I realized that I wasn't living up to the standards that God had for my life and that I needed to make a few changes. One change would include living a life of integrity and stopping the activities that prevented me from doing that, which meant giving up partying and drinking with my friends. It's crazy how many people fall out of your life when you stop living that way. But, I knew taking this one step would help me to LIVE again with vitality and energy and in a way, that would allow me to show people that I was living proof that my new lifestyle allows me to do way more to honor God. It also gave me the chance to have room in my life for newer, healthier, friendships that would help me continue living a life of integrity. These were people who would keep me in check and have a far greater influence in moving my life in the direction that God wants for me a whole lot faster. Once I realized how much faster I began moving in a positive direction with the right influences in my life, I started asking myself this question.

4. Am I getting advice from a biblically sound coach/mentor/pastor?

After seeing how much of an impact my counselor had on my life, I looked for a biblically sound life coach and even asked the pastor of my church to be my mentor. Mentors are great assets to your life. They tell you what you NEED to hear, not what you want to hear. They hold you accountable. They keep you in check, and most importantly, they help you realize that most of the things you are going through in your life aren't really as bad as you perceive them. Most of the time, mentors have already overcome these things and can offer you advice on how to overcome them much faster than they did. My counselor, my life coach, and my pastor are the three people I go to when I need advice, wisdom, and guidance. Having someone that can speak into my life and use God as the center gives me great insight when making tough decisions.

Are you asking yourself these same questions in your own life? If so, are you answering them honestly to allow yourself the opportunity to start working towards getting unstuck? Most importantly, are you willing to take action to make a change in your own life? Realizing that you are stuck but being unwilling to take action will leave you stuck. It is the actions you take that will create the biggest change in your life. You have to move. You can't anticipate moving, plan moving, and remain stationary. You have to get up and go. Even if you mess up, it's far better than never trying. What I have found in my personal life is that the biggest thing that blocked my path was me. I prevented myself from moving towards a life of integrity by not taking action to do the things that would help me get there. My fear of taking action prevented me from my future of reaching success faster. I didn't see that I had a problem that needed to be worked on and I thought I could solve my own problems. Upon receiving the help I needed from a biblical counselor, I began to realize that working on myself first was one of the best decisions I could have made. I was able to learn to love myself and clearly define what kind of people I would allow into my life. I learned how I was supposed to be treated in a relationship and what I was currently allowing that was unacceptable. I learned how to change my current approach and it started with me taking action and saying no to the bad friendships and relationships I knew weren't right for me. I recommend counseling to everyone, even if you don't think that you need it, because they can always help to offer you advice and a new perspective that you wouldn't be able to get elsewhere. You also have a sounding board who can help you see both sides of an issue from a healthy mindset, and if you seek a biblical counselor, they will help you remember to put God at the center of your life and remember to include him in all of your decisions, big or small. Once you're in a place where you can work on resolving your underlying issues, then you can begin using your story to help others. We will dig deeper into this in the last chapter. In the next chapter, I'm going to share some techniques that I used to help me restore my self-worth and confidence in myself. By using this technique, I was able to have a much stronger relationship with God and have the confidence I needed to let God use me to change the world.

What Blocks Your Path?

Chapter 3

Do You Remember to Look in the Mirror Every Day?

Do you ever find yourself comparing your life to other people who you perceive are better than you? You spend countless hours looking on social media, seeing only the best version of everyone's lives, feeling insignificant and paralyzed from stepping into your own purpose because you don't know if you could match up to any of the standards that you see. Well, I have some news for you.

This was me, a 28-year-old saleswoman who spent the majority of her career constantly comparing herself to the top performers, wondering what I was doing wrong, why I was never at the top, and why I worked so hard to only hit rock bottom every month. I constantly told myself that I wasn't good enough to get to that level, I didn't have the skill, I didn't have what it took, and that I didn't deserve the success I would receive once I got there, so I made barely enough money to pay my bills, but never enough to get ahead. I lived a life of constant scarcity. I was your typical struggling salesperson, barely scraping by to make ends meet, full of many excuses as to why my month didn't turn out how I expected. The economy was bad. There were not enough leads. The weather was bad. If there was an excuse, I probably used it. In the meantime, the top performers continued to rise, get better, and go beyond their limits. I was always curious as to what it was that made them different, why they were able to keep pushing when I was barely hanging on. What were they doing that I wasn't? Did they know something that I didn't know? What made the difference? I struggled for the longest time, until one day my eyes were opened in a way I never dreamed possible. This was the second turning point in my life.

I was driving home after yet another unfavorable day at the office when I passed a church that had a sign in the front that said, "I will not strive to be better than anyone, but better than I am today." What a great way to think, right? You are simply trying to beat your personal best each day. You are competing with only one person everyday…yourself. Reading that sign became a turning point in my life. My entire outlook about what it meant to be great was different and I hope my story can be a turning point for how to define greatness in your own life, too.

I began to look at my own life as a competition with myself. I'm a runner. What I love about running is that your ultimate goal is to strive to beat your personal best each time you run. You strive to beat one of your toughest competitors in every race, YOURSELF. Each time you pass your personal best, you strive to continue taking your skill to the next level. You don't worry about anyone around you. You just focus on yourself, which brings me to my next question.

What if you changed your approach? What if you put your focus on being the best version of yourself every day? What if you looked into the mirror and worked to be better than who you were yesterday? Did you know looking into the mirror could truly change your life? I read an article on Let's Reach Success, Turning Success into a Habit by Lidiya K, who wrote the book *The Mirror Technique*, that goes into greater detail about how to build confidence using this powerful exercise. The article teaches you about how to use your subconscious mind to appear and feel more confident in a matter of minutes. If you start by looking yourself in the mirror and speaking words that represent that you are the person you want yourself to be for 5-10 minutes a day, even if you are not there yet, over time, after 1-2 months of doing this every day, you will act, think, and become that person you keep telling yourself you are. I also heard a great speech by Zig Ziglar on the power of self-talk where he speaks about your eyes being the windows of your soul. He went on to tell a story about how he began to re-create his own positive self-image as an adult. He started by writing down the words I love myself 10 times, then he added the word 'because' after every sentence and filled in the blank with the reasons why he loved himself. The simple act of writing and saying this to himself every day began to change him in such a positive way. He noticed a big change in his confidence over time, which helped to shape him into the amazing role model that he was and changed the world in such a unique way. I'm not going to lie, it sounded silly to me when I first heard about these strategies. But, at a time where my confidence was the lowest and nothing else seemed to work, I decided to give it a try, as I had nothing to lose at this point. I was blown away as I began to see results almost right away. I noticed an immediate change with my sales at work, as they seemed to increase almost immediately. As I got more sales at work, that increased my confidence in my abilities even more. Then, that began to trickle over into other areas in my life. I began to become more certain about my abilities as a parent to create a better relationship with my son. That gave me more confidence in myself when it came to dating and I no longer accepted being treated unfairly in relationships, which guided me to begin attracting the right man into my life who later became my wonderful husband, Jeremy. Since I had confidence in myself, I was more confident in my relationship with God, and that is what I believe changed everything else in my life so rapidly. I would love to share some strategies with you that helped me. I encourage you to give it a try if you're ever in a place in your own life where you could use a confidence boost.

If you write down the words, "I love myself because _____" and fill in the blank and come up with 5-10 things that you love about yourself, then begin looking at yourself in the mirror and saying those things every night before bed for 30 days, you will notice a change in your confidence. If you have trouble coming up with some things that you love about yourself, try asking those around you that you love what they love about you. This may spark some ideas about qualities that you may begin to love that you never realized mattered. I didn't believe this at first, but I was desperate at a time in my life where my confidence was the lowest and decided I would try this to see if it worked. Here are some examples of some things I wrote down at the time to spark some ideas for you.

1. I love myself because God loves me.
2. I love myself because I am great at motivating others.
3. I love myself because I keep persisting when things get tough.
4. I love myself because I'm Awesome! You're welcome world.
5. I love myself because I'm a great mom. You're welcome Landon.
6. I love myself because I have an indispensable amount of energy.
7. I love myself because I'm in shape.
8. I love myself because I have amazing hair.
9. I love myself because I continue to get better and learn new things.
10. I love myself because I am smart.

What I discovered was a transformation that was so great, I was shocked. I began by saying the words I love myself because_____, but I didn't believe the things I spoke at first. After looking myself in the mirror and saying them for 30 days, what I found was that the words I spoke became my reality. It also got me in the habit of looking for more attributes that I loved about myself so I could re-do my list every 2 months. I also began doing this with my son. We would have family nights every 2 months or so where we would write down ten things that we loved about ourselves. If my son or I would struggle coming up with some things to say, we would start by giving each other ideas. You can also continue this in other ways as well. You can do this using your mirror as a reminder for you to stop, reflect, and say what you want in your life more than once per day. This is the strategy I followed.

Write down one thing, just one, that you want to become as if you have already done it.

> For example, if I wanted to be more confident with work and a top salesperson I would write:
> I have confidence in myself and an abundance of success at work.

Speak the words you write as if they already exist in your current life, even if they are not your reality yet. Write them down with a dry erase marker on a mirror that you pass by frequently throughout the day. I use my bathroom mirror and a mirror in my bedroom. Whenever you walk by that mirror, you look at yourself in the mirror and say whatever it is that you would like to claim out loud while you look yourself in the eye and walk away, like a boss! Drop the invisible mic if it makes you feel more excited. Make it a habit to do this every time you walk by the mirror and see how it begins to change your mind set about what's possible.

The third turning point that has been a game changer in my personal life was to define who I was as a woman of God. Once I found my identity in Christ, I was able to begin to see my purpose more clearly as the daughter of the ultimate king and therefore, live a more Christ-focused life. When I was intentional about developing a deeper relationship with Christ, I no longer needed to rely on other people's opinions of how I should live my life, because God had already decided that for me. I just needed to begin to listen to him and follow his lead.

Prior to that, I spent the majority of my life relying on other people to tell me who I was, what kind of values I had, and how my life was going to be lived out. After several months of being unhappy, depressed, and feeling stuck, I realized that I had been living my entire life on everyone else's terms and not mine. I was a product of who other people wanted me to be and this caused to me be indecisive and uncertain about everything in my life. I was living a life that was never mine. I felt that I had no purpose because I didn't create one for myself. But, I had to realize that I could not do this alone. I needed one very important person that would change everything for me: God.

This caused me to take time to sit down, write out, and design the life I wanted to live including God at the center of it. I had to ask myself, "If I were to die today, how would people remember me?" I came to the realization that I wasn't living a life at the time that I was proud to have people remember. I had to redesign my new life and take action towards making a small contribution every day that would leave the world a little better. It didn't have to be perfect, but I had to start. I started by doing a goal setting exercise where I set clear monthly, weekly, and daily goals that directed me toward having a life of purpose. The goals were aimed at making a difference in other people's lives. They included things like: buy someone coffee in the drive through, offer encouragement to someone who is having a tough time, compliment people who are working in the checkout lines at stores, call your parents and tell them you love them, leave your spouse a note expressing your appreciation for the things they do that may seem that you overlook, and making sure people know that they matter and that they make a positive difference in your life. It's really hard to feel depressed when you're making a positive difference in other people's lives around you. This was what I wanted to be remembered for, helping people see that they matter. How do you want people to remember you? Today is your day to start taking action towards the things that you are called to do and begin working towards having the life you have deserved all along.

The fourth turning point that was a BIG game changer in my life was being intentional in having time to be with God. This could be done in several ways. I personally love to sing worship music when I run, as it helps me feel a much deeper connection with God while simultaneously getting healthy. Yes, I did say sing while I run. Singing while running may sound a lot harder than it is, however, it creates a bit of a challenge for me as my running pace has to be consistent enough to allow me to have enough air to belt out the words in those songs. If I am able to sing while I run, I know I am running at the right pace to allow me to connect with God, therefore, giving me a larger purpose to run for: my God. It also gives me a sense of joy that re-energizes my excitement for the things that God has in store for my future. The Bible speaks of this re-energizing in Psalm 51:12 where it says, "Restore to me the joy of your salvation, and make me willing to obey you." I love running outdoors and getting to feel the presence of God while enjoying nature. There's something about having peace, quietness, tranquility, and alone time with God that changes my heart towards the unfavorable things that may happen in my life. It allows for God to speak to me and for me to have the time to listen. My mind is still and my heart is ready to receive his word. I am ready to start my day off right with God by my side.

I also love to be involved in doing Bible studies at my church. It helps me continue to learn more about the character of God and hear other people talk about the things they are going through in their own lives. It reminds me that I am not alone with some of the battles I may be facing and gives me good Scripture references for when I am going through tough times. Plus, I get to connect with some really amazing people who love God as much as I do. I have noticed that when I take time to be intentional in creating a relationship with God, things seem to flow a little easier in my personal life. It doesn't mean things are perfect, but dealing with the imperfect times in my life tends to be a lot easier when my relationship with

God is solid. This only happens when I take time out of my day to create a relationship with God, to talk to God, to involve God in my everyday decisions, and to run with God. Whatever helps you connect with God, I want to encourage you to be intentional in your own life towards building a deeper relationship with Him. I believe that God wants us to look in the mirror every day and imagine that he is behind that mirror cheering us on, encouraging us, and showing us the love we deserve to receive from our father. I believe that if we take time to look in the mirror and not only remind ourselves that our lives are worth living but that they can have significant purpose if we will allow God to be a part of our lives more.

Will you remember to look in the mirror today?

Chapter 4

How Do You Develop Faith from Failure?

Do you like to deal with challenges? If you are like most people, the answer is more than likely NO. Challenges require you to deal with the reality that we all like to pretend doesn't exist. We paralyze ourselves with a fake reality. Think about it. We spend the majority of our life posting pictures of our perfect lives on social media, pretending that we have it all together. When we run into people, we wear a mask showcasing that we are this invincible superhero who is great at everything and has no flaws, while secretly, we are a complete mess on the inside. We hide the emotions that require us to deal with our problems. We spend so much time wearing a mask and we let so many challenges pile up that by this point, we are afraid of ourselves and what we would be forced to deal with if we actually did acknowledge our challenges. Then, we do nothing. However, by hiding our emotions, we are depriving ourselves of growth. We have grown into a society of people who are afraid to be authentic with their shortcomings and avoid challenging situations because it's too much to deal with, we don't know how to deal with it, or we simply don't have the right mindset about what it means to take on a challenge in a positive way. This brings me to my first point.

In order for us to realize that challenges are good, we must first change our mindset about what it means to take on a challenge. Challenges can be your greatest obstacle, as well as your greatest source of strength. They take you to a deep place inside where you are forced to gain wisdom and change. Is it tough? YES. Is it Hard? YES. But, is it REQUIRED in order for you to grow? Absolutely. Some of my greatest challenges have propelled me in a direction that has changed my life in a very positive way. This brings me to my next point.

We have to find a way to find pleasure in the pain. There are several instances where this happens throughout the Bible. When Paul writes about the many trials he has faced in his life, he states, "That's why I take pleasure in my weakness, and in the insults, hardships, persecutions, and troubles that I suffer for Christ. For when I am weak, then I am strong. (2 Corinthians 12:9-10) Paul chose to focus on the good, on God's grace, instead of the trials he had to overcome.

Around a similar time, James, the brother of Jesus, wrote in a letter, "When troubles of any kind come your way, consider it an opportunity for great joy. For when your faith is tested, your endurance has a chance to grow. So let it grow, for when your endurance is fully developed, you will be perfect and complete, needing nothing." (James 1:2-4) James decided to view troubled times as an opportunity for personal growth to look more like Christ.

As Paul instructs the Romans on the benefits of believing in Christ, he states, "We can rejoice, too, when we run into problems and trials, for we know that they help us develop endurance. And endurance develops strength of character, and character strengthens our confident hope of salvation." (Romans 5:3-5) Paul viewed going through tribulations as an opportunity to prepare his people to have everlasting joy.

One way that has worked in my personal life is getting a journal and looking for the challenges that happen, overcoming them, and then writing about how I felt before the challenge and how I felt after I surpassed the challenge. It doesn't have to be very long, mine were typically one page. But, every time I had a challenge that I faced, big or small, I wrote about my fears before and what I learned in the midst of conquering my challenge. Then, when I faced a challenge in the future, I would refer to my stories of overcoming obstacles in the past and overtime it would become easier to move forward.

Fast forward to age 28; I was struggling desperately at my job. I was broke. I counted every penny I spent everywhere I went. As a single parent, I spent most of my nights crying myself to sleep wondering how I was going to pay my bills that month. I told myself that I wasn't worthy of success. Quite honestly, I never knew what success looked like or believed it was possible for me, personally. But one day I hit my breaking point. I was so furious. I knew success could be possible for me. I knew I had better skill, motivation, and drive than half of the people that I observed who were already achieving success. I was so tired of giving up in my life. I was tired of doubting myself. I was tired of holding myself back from the things I knew I was capable of doing. I was sick of failing over and over. I was sick of seeing results that I knew were not an adequate representation of me at my best. Most importantly, I was tired of being at the bottom. I felt like the biggest failure in my career. In fact, I don't know how I even kept my job with the results I was producing some months. So, I started praying a very specific but simple prayer multiple times a day. I said, "God, will you take me beyond the limits that I put on myself?" Every time I would feel discouraged or sense doubt creeping in like a bad virus, I would say this prayer. I lived this prayer. I became this prayer. I said this prayer so much that it was almost as if it was who I was becoming, a person who would go beyond any limits that they have ever put on themselves. For the first time in my life, I let go of all my fears and limitations that I put on myself and gave it all to God. I let go and let God take complete control of my life.

How do many of us do this? We have a great idea or get inspired, then stop because we make up some excuse as to why we can't accomplish it. Meanwhile, we are secretly dying on the inside because we aren't going after the things in our lives that truly excite us. We stop living for God and start living for what we believe we are supposed to be in society. We work mundane jobs that give us no meaning.

We are involved in so many activities that we have no time to slow down and be present. Most importantly, we miss the opportunities that God puts right in front of us that could potentially bring us more joy, more excitement, and more fulfillment.

Have you ever been in a place in your life where you are sick of where you are? You have been climbing the mountaintop for long enough and you are ready to be at the top. You are ready to dominate. You are ready to let your inner greatness come out and to show the world what you are truly capable of. You're ready for a BIG change. Relying on God to show me what I was capable of was a big leap of faith for me. I didn't even believe in myself and my own abilities, how was I going to believe in what God could do for me? Asking God in prayer to take me beyond the limits I was putting on myself began to have a tremendous impact on my life.

Prior to that month of asking God to take me beyond the limits I had put on myself, I had never sold more than 15 cars in one month. I didn't believe I was capable, it was a mental limit that I had put on myself, and I didn't trust God to take over where I wasn't capable. But, I decided that nothing else was working so I decided to give it to God and ask for his help. My goal was to sell 20 cars that month, so I began by asking God to take me beyond the limits that I kept putting on myself and help me get to 20 cars that month. I asked him to bring me people that he knew I could help and that he knew I would work well with given my current abilities and skills. Every time I was feeling like I wasn't good at my job or I didn't have the skill I needed or I didn't have what it took, I prayed the same prayer and asked God the same question, "God, will you take me beyond the limits that I put on myself?" I wanted to see further, but I couldn't. However, I knew God could and I relied on him as if he was the water I needed to drink to keep me alive. I trusted in him in a way I never trusted in him before. For the first time in my life, I let God take the reins and took a step back, which was not easy coming from a person who likes to be in control of EVERYTHING. Relying on God in this way taught me something far greater than I could have ever learned had I not taken this chance and had faith. It taught me that you don't put limits on what God is capable of doing through you. He doesn't accept your goals as his goals. He can and will take you further than you ever dreamed possible if you will just let him. That month I sold the most cars I have ever sold in my entire career, 26 cars in one month! I'm definitely not implying that if you ask God for more money or more success that he will answer your prayer like this every time. However, I did learn that if you put your faith in God, let him take the reins, and follow him, the doors of success will be opened and you can and will go beyond any limits that you have ever put on yourself. Proverbs 16:3 says, "Commit your actions to the lord and your plans will succeed."

So, what are you willing to ask God to help you with today?

Are you willing to trust him and ask until you see his result and not yours? I challenge you to begin by asking God and seeing how he transforms your life.

How Do You Develop Faith from Failure?

Chapter 5

How Running from God, Brought Me Closer to God

This is the story of a teenage girl who grew up to be a successful business-woman and struggled with fear, doubt, and a low self-image for the first thirty years of her life. She had many relationships that were unsuccessful because she let her pride get in the way. She didn't want to admit that she had a very low self-image and quite honestly didn't see any issues with herself, as everyone else around her was to blame for the things that went wrong in her life, not her. She didn't accept responsibility for the things that she knew she needed to change because then that would require her to take action to change them. She let God come in and out of her life when it was convenient for her. She never quite knew what it meant to truly give everything to God and to trust him. This girl was me. Lost, confused, and always running away from my problems instead of facing them head on. My relationship with God hasn't always been perfect. I ran away from God more times than I could count, but through his forgiveness, I was saved and eventually started running to God. This is where my story begins.

I ran away from God hoping to escape the things I never wanted to face. I thought that running away would eventually cause my struggles to disappear and that I would no longer have to worry about them anymore. What I didn't realize was that the farther I ran from God, the more I needed God. The more I tried to avoid God, the more clearly he made his presence in my life. I ran and God chased after me with the intention to save me, much like he is doing to every single one of us. The more I gave up on myself, the more God showed up in my corner. The faster I ran, the quicker God was there. I couldn't begin to fathom a God that loved me so much that he refused to give up on me no matter what. I didn't have that example in my life growing up. It was so hard to grasp the fact that I had a God who was willing to go to great lengths to show me he truly loved and cared about me. I didn't want to believe it. I didn't want to see the signs that God kept putting in front of me. However, he never gave up on me and I'm glad we serve a God that doesn't give up because it actually brought me closer to God.

I was a single parent who had just graduated from college with a degree in Neuroscience. I was the first person in my family to graduate from college and that was a huge accomplishment. My plan was to go to medical school and pursue pediatric neurosurgery and become our family's first doctor, but that meant that I would have to rely on someone else to raise my son, as medical school would be very demanding of my time and leave me little time to be a present parent. I had a decision to make and I knew it was going to be a hard one. I had wanted to go to medical school since I was in the 6th grade. It was the only plan I had for my life. I didn't have a backup plan, but I knew this would take me away from raising my son the way I wanted to raise him. Therefore, I decided to focus on raising him instead.

This was when I began to hit a downward spiral. Since I had no clue what I wanted to do with my life, I remained a server at the same restaurant that I worked at in college. I was unhappy and unfulfilled at this job, so I felt stuck. Instead of doing anything about it, I took my mind off of dealing with it by drinking with people after work to justify my decision of staying complacent because they were stuck in their own lives. Since I filled my spare time outside of working with drinking and socializing and my mornings sleeping, I was not a very present parent, therefore, I was in the same boat I would have been had I decided to go to medical school. I didn't go to church because I worked on Sundays and my relationship with God was non-existent. I knew I needed to change but I had no idea what to do next. It was in that time in my life that God decided to step in and help.

I was going into work like any other night and waited on what I would determine to be the worst table of human beings on the planet. It was a group of five very demanding people, who took up so much of my time that I was unable to successfully help my other tables around me. I was running around like a crazy person working as hard as I could to fulfil the seemingly never-ending needs of everyone at this table. At the end of their meal, when I passed out their checks, not only did they not leave me a tip, but they didn't leave me enough money to pay for their meal, which I didn't realize until after they had already left. I was devastated. I worked so hard to provide great service for a table of people who seemed as if they didn't appreciate it. Tears began to fill my eyes as the thoughts of being a struggling single parent who counted on every tip to provide for her child began to go through my mind. It was at that moment that I realized that I needed to change. I had officially hit my breaking point. I could no longer continue living this life anymore.

Sometimes God has a funny way of guiding you down a different path, which is exactly what he did that night. I was complacent, even though I knew I wasn't living my best version of myself, and I had no reason to want to make the change. God knew I needed change because he had something better for me. I didn't want to listen so he helped me see that change needed to happen. As I look back on that night, which seemed to be the worst night of my life at the time, I thank God for his persistence because if he had not shown me the pain of staying complacent, I would have never experienced the pleasure of moving on to the better things that God had in store for me. Now I had a decision to make. What was next for me? I had no clue, but I knew anything had to be better than my job at the time. I'm not discounting that being a server is a bad position as I think it gave me a new appreciation for how to treat people. I have a new rule that I will always tip my server 20% no matter what because I never know what they are going through and I understand that they count on their tips to live. However, for me, this job was at a place in my life that caused me to stay complacent and justify my poor decisions by getting wrapped up in the lifestyle of going out drinking with co-workers after work and simply not living a life that was in my best interest, so it wasn't good for me to stay. But, now what?

I began interviewing for a pharmaceutical sales company that encouraged me to work in a sales position for a few months in order to get the experience that I needed for them to hire me, so I began to search and apply for some sales positions. I ended up landing a job as a management trainee for a great company that promoted me based off of my performance. That resulted in me becoming a branch manager within a little over a year with the company. A few short months later, I was promoted to sell cars for the same company. I worked during the day, which kept me too busy to have time to go out with my old co-workers at night, so I was able to be home with my son and we began going back to church. This was the beginning of my journey of finding myself and digging deeper into my relationship with God.

The relationships with my old co-workers began to diminish and I began to fill my spare time being a greeter at church on Sunday mornings and joining a women's Bible study during the week. I wanted to be involved with everything I could to grow deeper in my relationship with God. Then, I heard a leader from our church speak about how our church serves on a mission trip to Costa Rica every year. I began to get really excited about this possible opportunity that I could now be a part of with our church. I had always wanted to go on a mission trip, but could never afford it. But, I felt a strong tug on my heart that I needed to go and that this was my time to make that commitment. I was excited, but very nervous about making this decision. I was just barely making enough money to survive at the time, as I was still struggling to discover my true potential at work. To be honest, it didn't make sense financially for me to be able to go, but I put down the initial deposit of $50, bought less groceries that week, and decided that I needed to trust that God would help me. I spent the rest of the week racking my brain about how I could come up with the rest of the money for this trip. Finally, I decided to pray and ask God for help and trust him. That was when I got a phone call that changed my life.

The pastor of my church gave me a call. He said, "This doesn't happen very often, but someone came to the church just now and wanted to anonymously pay for your entire trip to Costa Rica." I remember my eyes filling up with tears and being so grateful in that moment. I knew it was God taking care of me. It was like he was showing me that if I follow his path, he will provide a way. I spent that entire week prior to getting that phone call doubting my own abilities of coming up with the money to make this possible when I should have been trusting in God's ability to make it happen.

This mission trip was exactly what I needed to start over in my life. I had just gotten out of another unhealthy relationship and had decided for the first time in my life to give it all to God. I had struggled with co-dependency most of my life.

I had to have someone by my side to rely on all the time. This would keep me in bad relationships longer than I needed because I was afraid of being alone. I had functioned in co-dependent relationships for so long that I didn't even know who I was anymore. I couldn't make my own decisions and I had lost my identity as an individual person. My identity would always include the traits of whoever I was dating at the time and I never felt like I was my own person. After seeking counseling and beginning the process of working on myself, I decided to take some time off from dating. I was the loneliest I had ever been in my life during this season. I spent a lot of nights crying myself to sleep and praying for God to help me not feel so alone. A week before the mission trip, I had accepted that I needed to take some time to work on me and decided to give my relationship problems to God to handle. I decided, for the first time in my life, to let God show me the way and if I needed to be single for a while, I was going to be ok with that because God would know exactly what to do to help me in my journey. This trip was my start over, my acceptance to the things that God had for me, and my beginning to the type of relationship that God wanted me to have in my life.

The first few days of the mission trip were incredible. I had no access to my phone, so it was nice to finally have some time to simply be myself. I was excited and re-energized. I was present to the things around me in a world where family time was of utmost importance and relationships with other people were a priority. I didn't speak Spanish very well, but going on this trip taught me that you don't need to speak the same language to show people that you care about them. Actions speak louder than words and hugs are the greatest gifts that you can give to the younger kids, who sometimes are never shown any affection in their homes. It gave me a greater appreciation for the things I took for granted at home. It made me realize that I needed to get outside of myself and focus on the bigger picture and my contribution to the world. I realized that my problems were so small compared to the things going on in our world. I met a group of people who were genuinely happy with little when I had spent my entire life being dissatisfied with a lot. They made the best of what they had and getting to know Jesus had been the greatest blessing in their lives, when I didn't slow down enough to appreciate his blessing in my own life. It made me realize that I needed to focus on being present in my life. I needed to slow down and be grateful for how far I had come in my life. I needed to appreciate the little things along the way.

As the mission trip was coming to an end, we went to Jaco beach to debrief and process all of our emotions to deal with them as much as we could before we headed back to our normal lives again. We talked, we cried, and we prayed, but we also got to enjoy some of the most beautiful sunrises and sunsets that I have ever seen in my life. I'm a sucker for beautiful sunrises and sunsets and anytime I am near a beach, I love to go for a nice run. I enjoy running with waves crashing, the ocean breeze on my face, and miles of sand and ocean in my horizon. It reminds me that with God, anything is possible.

We were sitting around the pool admiring the beach when I mentioned that I wanted to go for a run in the morning to watch the sunrise. I asked if anyone would like to join, in which the majority of the crowd laughed and one person spoke up and said, "I'll go with you!" It was Jeremy. He was relatively new to our church so I didn't know a lot about him, other than the fact that he was my good friend Amy's cousin. I met Amy at my sister's birthday party a year prior. I had just started going to church at the time and was so excited about how quickly my life had changed since God was a part of it. I began by telling her story after story about my transformation. She had never experienced what I had experienced in church and asked if she could come to church with me. I honestly didn't tell her my stories with that intent. I was just really proud of how far I'd come in such a short amount of time with God by my side and I wanted to tell everyone who would listen. But, God had other plans. Amy came to our church the following Sunday. She recommitted her life to the Lord and was baptized a few months later.

Amy began serving Jesus by working with the youth. She became an integral part of our church family. She was so excited about the things that God was doing in her life that now she wanted to share her excitement with anyone who would listen. She would constantly update her social media about the new and exciting things that were happening in her life with God now part of it. It's always hard to tell if sharing your story makes a difference, but it does. When you think people aren't watching the way you live your life, they are and this is where Jeremy came into her life.

Jeremy and Amy were cousins, but as they grew older and began living different lives, they didn't get to see each other as much. Jeremy was a manager at a bar, living a life consumed with drinking and partying. Jeremy always knew he wanted something better for his life, but didn't know where to find it. He was stuck. He was never a crazy person when he drank and he wasn't loud or obnoxious, so from the public's eye, it didn't seem like he had a problem, but he did. That problem resulted in him getting into his car and driving home one night with no recollection of ever getting there. He woke up the next morning confused and unsure of how he got home, only to realize that he had driven himself and did not remember it at all. Although no one was hurt from this instance, it was Jeremy's breaking point. He realized that he could have easily killed someone by his careless actions and knew he had hit rock bottom. It was Sunday morning. He had seen Amy's posts and watched her life transform with God and immediately called her. He said, "I see what you have and I want that, can I come to church with you this morning?" Amy very excitedly said yes and was so happy to see her cousin want to embark on the same journey with her. Jeremy walked into church that day and left a different man. He hasn't touched alcohol since.

He began getting involved in everything he could in church, which led him to helping out with cook-outs at the church youth outings. He heard Amy talk about the Costa Rica mission trip and wanted to be a part of it. Unfortunately, they book up almost a year in advance so the chance of him being able to go were very slim. A few weeks later, one of the people scheduled to go to Costa Rica suddenly had to cancel and Jeremy signed up right away. Jeremy's story was always such an interesting and incredible testimony, so when he mentioned that he wanted to go run in Costa Rica, I was excited to get to know him better. I immediately asked him with excitement, "You run?" He replied, "Yeaaaaaaa!" Truth be told, he was not a runner and hadn't run in a really long time. He kept up with me really well that morning, but secretly he thought his heart was going to come out of his chest. He just played it off really well.

That run was a great opportunity for me to get to know him a little better. He was raised by a single mom and understood how difficult it was to raise a child on your own. He came from a blended family that didn't get along for the first part of his life. He told me about how an emergency surgery that he had to have brought his family together and from that moment on they decided to look past their differences and make it work for their family. He told me about his dreams about having his own family and wanting to work as hard as he could to show his kids a different path. He talked about how he appreciated what he had gone through in his life because it made him the man he is today. He told me about his sister who passed away from a brain aneurism unexpectedly a few years ago and how that caused him to drink more. That started his downward spiral and eventually his breaking point. He realized that he was not living a life that he was proud of. He wanted something different and that's what caused him to go to church that day and eventually on his first mission trip.

I remember feeling so amazed at Jeremy's drive, ambition, and determination to seek a relationship with God. He was proud of his decision and happy to be on this new journey in his life. Jeremy had spent his entire life running away from God and now he was running towards the things that God had in store for him with the biggest grin on his face, ready to take on the world. He didn't look back on his past mistakes. He didn't let that define him. He simply accepted it, appreciated that his decisions took him to where he is today, and loved God with all of his heart. I didn't tell him at the time, but he was everything I had ever wanted in a man. I didn't go on the mission trip to find love. I went to find myself. In the midst of finding myself, I found God and in the midst of serving God, I found a man who would walk right beside me serving God every step of the way. I found Jeremy. In the most unlikely place, in the most unlikely circumstance, on a trip that he wasn't supposed to be able to even go on, God brought me Jeremy. I was away from all of the distractions of my world back home that would have kept me from being present and getting to know him. I was in a place where I went without make up, cute clothes, and warm showers. I was stripped from everything that covered up my imperfections and was myself in my purest form. Through it all, Jeremy still pursued me. He proposed to me a year later in front of all the people who went with us on that Costa Rica mission trip and we were married five months later.

It's funny how God works in our lives when we trust in him. He gives us everything we could have ever wanted and more. We have the choice to trust. We have the choice to follow. We have the choice to go. God always leaves the choice to us. I've run away from God and been able to achieve things in my life with a much more difficult path. I've run towards God and had things seemingly fall into my path. I'm not implying that this is the case all the time. However, it has definitely been the case more times when I run toward God than when I run away. I don't believe that God wants to make our life difficult, but he does have to teach us, and sometimes we can be very stubborn. However, when you truly decide to give it all to God and trust him, he will open doors for you that you would never see coming.

I was a single parent with no hope, and God brought me hope through a song at church. I was struggling with the relationships in my life, and God brought me a husband who honored and respected me. Now, as I struggle to write this book, be vulnerable, and tell my story about my journey back to God, I hope that it encourages you to discover and create your own journey so that you can share it with other people and inspire them. Nobody's story is the same, which is the beauty in your journey. But, if you are not sharing it, you are doing yourself and the world a disservice because you never know whose life you are missing out on making a difference in by not taking action. There are so many social media platforms that are available at our fingertips today. They are a great way to share your story to the most amount of people.

You can also get involved with your local church and find out where you can plug in and start inspiring people with your story. There may be groups that you can join or places in your local community that you can offer to speak at to begin. If you like to write, you can begin by starting a blog. However you feel is the easiest way for you, I would like to encourage you to start by asking yourself these three questions:

1. Have I ever run away from God?
2. How did it bring me closer to God?
3. How can I share my story with the world?

And then start making a difference in people's lives today.

Chapter 6

Are You Afraid to Go Deeper?

I spent the majority of my life being a funny, outgoing, person who constantly craved attention and acceptance. I was truly a little bit of an introvert, but I trained myself to be extraverted as it got me the acceptance I craved and helped me build what I perceived to be my identity. Little did I know that my identity was a direct reflection of what other people wanted me to be and not an accurate depiction of who I truly was, but the attention and acceptance became a huge source of what I felt I needed in order to be known in the world. People loved being around me because they never knew what to expect. It was almost like I was a clown in a circus, constantly performing. It was fun when I was out with crowds of people, but then as the night would end, I would come home and feel so alone, defeated, and lost.

As I got to college, my loneliness began to be filled with alcohol, perceived friendships, and crazier nights that ended up with me drinking until I would pass out. I began to see a direct reflection of my parents in my actions and behaviors and this became my wake-up call.

I knew at this point in my life, I had two choices: I could go down the path that my parents took and live a life of constant stress and disappointment, or I could do one of the hardest things I thought could ever be done and change it! I had no idea what that looked like at the time, but I knew I had to stop living a lie. I had to start living my life on my terms. I had to start being the best version of me every single day. I had to be the change that my family never dreamed was possible. I had to be that example and to do that, I had to begin.

I'm not going to say this journey was easy, but I will say it was the best decision I could have made in my life. I lived a surface-level life and had what I perceived to be genuine friendships. What I came to realize was that these friendships were not real. They did not go deep. I kept people at arm's length, only telling them what I wanted them to know and not getting close with people. It was my way of protecting myself from not getting hurt. I was secretly afraid to go deeper. I spent so much of my life building my identity on what others wanted me to be that I was afraid that if I revealed my true self to the world, I wouldn't be accepted. I knew I needed help and if I really wanted to see a dramatic change, I could no longer rely on myself for all the answers. I had to go down a different path. This path required me to humble myself. I had to drop the pride that I had formed over many years that prevented me from going further because I had convinced myself that I had it all together and I didn't need any help. For the first time in my life, I asked for help from an EXPERT, which leads me to my next point.

Who do you reach out to when you are going through a tough time? Are the people you reach out to building you back up or agreeing with your excuses that you tell them of why your life is "oh so hard"?

If you are reaching out to people who agree with your excuses and give you more validation as to why your excuses are fine, you might want to consider changing the people you allow to influence you. I struggled with this for a good part of my life. I would take parenting advice from people who weren't parents. I would get relationship advice from people who couldn't keep a steady relationship. I would get sales advice from underperformers and wonder why I was failing at every avenue in my life. Do you see the problem here? As my life coach Mike Rodriguez always says, "Never take advice from someone more messed up than you are." I did this for so long that I was SUCCEEDING very well at FAILING because I allowed the wrong people to give me advice that didn't add real value to my life. This is why it is so imperative to protect who you allow to speak into your life and make sure they are successful in the area that you are hoping to get advice about in your own life. Once I started doing this, I noticed a big change in my personal life and here's how I started.

I began by getting a Christian counselor, as I was looking to gain a better perspective on what a healthy relationship looked like and how to get out of the endless cycle of dating the wrong people and feeling like there were no more good guys in the world. I used to think that I attracted crazy people and that healthy relationships didn't exist except for in movies. What I came to realize was that you attract what you are and what you allow into your life. Through counseling, I came to realize that I allowed people to treat me the way I shouldn't be treated and therefore attracted the wrong people by allowing them into my life. I didn't defend myself if they talked down to me. I allowed them to tell me what I wanted and became codependent, relying on the person I was dating to make decisions for me. I lost my identity and became the person I was dating. I wasn't my own person anymore and wondered why I was depressed and felt like I had no purpose. After seeking counseling, I realized that I had to re-define what I wanted out of life on MY terms. I had to have my own goals outside of the person I was dating. I had to slowly start to remold the clay that I let others shape me into for years and become the mold of who I wanted to be instead. I had to work on me before I could take my life to the next level. I had to look in the mirror and admit that it was time for me to be the solution to my own problems. This caused me to progress even further.

Having a counselor helped give me the confidence I needed to admit that I wasn't an expert at everything in my life. However, it made me humble enough to not be afraid to ask for help. When I wanted to take my work life to the next level, I reached out to my group manager at work to ask for help. When my spiritual life wasn't where I needed it to be, I reached out to the pastor of my church. When I was ready to go further with every aspect of my life, I got a life coach. I went straight to the top and looked for the experts in the field that I wanted to excel in. I was pleasantly surprised to find out that most of these experts who I was so afraid to ask for advice from were very pleased to share their experiences, advice, and ways that they overcame their own struggles. It made me realize that I was not alone and that other people have been down a similar path. It also made me realize that I was able to climb out of the hole of doubts and into the sky of possibilities that I never knew were feasible in my life.

As I close out this chapter, I want to leave you with two questions to think about:

1) Have you ever asked someone to be your mentor?
2) If not, Why?

I would encourage you to look around and find the people in your life who are DOMINATING in an area of their lives that you would love to get better at and ask them to coffee or lunch. Ask them how they got started, what struggles they had to face, and how they got to where they are today. I challenge you to begin today and watch your life transform in a way you never dreamed possible.

Are You Afraid to Go Deeper?

Chapter 7

Why Does God Need You to Move?

Have you ever found yourself in a place in your life where you know you need to make a change but you don't? You're afraid. You're comfortable. You don't want to have uncertainty about your future. Or you just don't know what that next move needs to be. You are stuck. You are stationary. You are stranded. Well, God does not bring us to this earth to do nothing with our lives. He wants us to take action and trust that he will work out the details. God wants to help us put our own puzzle together, but WE must buy the puzzle, take it out of the box, and begin placing the pieces that fit together in their proper arrangements. We have to take initiative and start. Then, God will come in beside us to connect the rest of the pieces and help us see the finished picture. In order to begin taking action on the things God has in store for you, God needs you to move. It was in the place that I stood still that held me back from living a life of true purpose, but during this time I learned the greatest lesson to help me propel toward my destiny.

I was determined that it would get better. I was determined to fight through. I wanted to find the solution to this misery so I could teach other people how to get through it in their own lives. I was making more money than I ever had in my life. I let that money motivate me to stay in a place where I wasn't growing longer than I should. I spent most nights crying on my drive home from work, with a feeling that I was trapped with no other options. I was told that I would never find a job that paid as well as my current job. I was told that all work places were filled with unhappy people. I was told that the grass wasn't really greener on the other side. I let the beliefs of the people who were stuck in their own lives hold me back from moving forward in mine. I slowly became just like those people. Truth be told, I hated where I was in my life. I was stuck at a job filled with people who were complacent and could no longer give me answers to the questions that I needed to get to the next level. It was a place filled with managers who celebrated complacency, who avoided dealing with difficult situations, and who hated their own jobs. I was stuck and afraid to make a move because I didn't see my own potential. I didn't realize what I was really capable of doing so I remained in that lonely place, working a job that was unfulfilling, and began to slip into a state of depression.

During this time, I was just getting back into church and struggling to figure out where I stood with my faith, therefore, I distanced myself from God. In fact, I didn't talk to God at all. I was mad at him for not giving me instant gratification and having the next best thing fall into my lap when I needed it. How many of us do this?

We live in a society where we expect things to happen right away and expect God to give us instant results on OUR terms. What I discovered was that when you distance yourself from God, you are left more vulnerable and more susceptible to believe the lies that satan wants you to believe so he can hold you back from the things that God has in store for you. satan wants you to believe that you are not capable of doing great things because then you don't take action to do the things that serve God. You do nothing and serve satan. By doing nothing, you are letting satan have control of your life. You are letting him help you justify why the negative thoughts you have about yourself are slowly becoming your reality. But, God doesn't want us to remain in the desert, doing nothing to impact the world. He needs us to move.

This brings me to the story in Exodus in the Bible where God was directing the Israelites to the land of milk and honey. The Israelites had lived a very hard life of constant struggle and God wanted the opportunity to show them the better life that they were capable of having if they would simply TRUST him. God asked for nothing more than for them to follow him and trust him. He had no catch. He just wanted to show them that when you move in obedience, he will follow through on his promises and provide you with things you could never provide yourself with on your own. He wanted to open up a better path, an easier path for these people to consider. All he needed was their faith, trust, and movement. Our God is a very simple God and I think we tend to complicate God's intentions for our lives into something that is much harder than what he really wants for us. God doesn't expect us to be a perfect superhuman with a check list of orders from him. He doesn't operate using "To Do" lists with tedious tasks for us to complete before he will help us. Our God prefers "To Go" options instead. You see, when God puts something on your heart, it is your time to go. You must move towards the things he has called you to do, faithfully.

For the Israelites, the land of milk and honey was a desired place for them to live as it had fertile land that would provide them with plenty of food and a life of luxurious living compared to their current circumstances. This land would be their well-deserved breakthrough and God was ready to show them that they could live a much better life if they would just follow him. God sent the Israelites to take possession of the land that he had promised them. He told them that they were perfectly capable of defeating the current inhabitants of the land. He was like their coach, giving them the exact play that he knew would help them score the goal that would cause them to win the game, but they doubted, they lost faith, and therefore, they didn't move. In order for God to create a better tomorrow for their future, he needed them to follow through. He couldn't be the only one holding up to his end of the deal. He relies on us to do his work on earth. It's a two-way street. We have faith, God follows through. We trust, God delivers. We move, God shows us a better way. Since they stayed still and did nothing, God did not yet fulfill his promise. God was not happy about this and he cursed them with forty years of wandering in the wilderness until that entire generation who lacked belief in God's abilities died off. Through their unbelief, they were unable to accomplish great things through God on this earth. They lived lives of mediocrity and left no impact in the world. They were wandering generalities who left the earth with nothing memorable behind because they didn't take action.

So why does God need us to move? Because we are not brought to this earth to stand still. It is our duty to make a difference in as many lives as possible. Our lives would remain unchanged, uneventful, and unfulfilled if we remained complacent, and God wants so much more for us. I had to move in my own life to begin seeing God's work being done through me.

I stayed at my job feeling unfulfilled because I thought I was stuck, I refused to trust God, and I refused to see the opportunities in front of me. I decided to stop believing that God had a use for me in my current position. I didn't trust that God could still use me in my place of waiting. Therefore, I stopped taking action to move towards the greater purpose that God had for my life. But, God has a nice way of getting through to you, even when you don't talk to him. This time it was through someone else that really knew how to get my attention.

I had a customer who had come to see me several months prior, show up out of the blue. Months ago, this customer told me she was just looking at cars that day but would come back to see me at a later date when she was ready, as she had to get some financial stuff in order first. Now being in car sales, I hear this quite a bit from customers who I never see after that conversation, but I proceeded to spend some time helping to show this customer all of the details of several car options and answer all of her questions to help her narrow down her options. I never expected to see her back, but I knew I had done everything I could do to help her that day. Now, here she was, excited to see me and ready to buy a car, just like she had promised several months back. I was struck with curiosity as to what propelled her to come back to see me. That is when she said, "I went to several car dealerships months ago when I was trying to decide where I wanted to go to purchase my vehicle. I prayed and asked God where he wanted me to go and God told me to come see you. I always listen to my God, so here I am." I was speechless. Here I was, stuck in my own negative thoughts, feeling like I wasn't making an impact, and therefore walking endlessly in a desert doing nothing while I was stuck, just like the Israelites, when God used this customer to show me that I had been making a difference all along, even in my place of waiting. No matter where you are in your life, God will always find a way to use you. He does not give up on you because you have given up on yourself. He does not need you to have the perfect life, ideal situation, or dream job to be ready to use you. God is ready to use you right where you are and he's not afraid to use you when you feel like you are at your worst because your worst could be the best thing that happens to someone else's life.

In 2 Corinthians 12:9-10, God Says, "'My Grace is all you need. My power works best in your weakness.' That's why I take pleasure in my weaknesses, and in the insults, hardships, persecutions, and troubles that I suffer for Christ. For when I am weak, then I am strong." God needs you to take action, get up, and move in order to make a difference. So, I would like to end the chapter with these two questions:

1. What can you do today to move towards the thing God is calling you to do?
2. Are you willing to start today?

Now go and begin to move and watch how God transforms your life.

Why Does God Need You to Move?

Chapter 8

How Do You Accept God's Forgiveness?

I thought that sharing my story would help me to get rid of the heavy burden of feeling unworthy because of the decisions I made in my past. This was my healing and my breakthrough. Although sharing my story offered me a great sense of relief, I still carried a giant weight with me every day that I struggled to get rid of. This weight was a result of the thoughts that I told myself over and over and were the greatest detriment to my complete healing. I held onto the thoughts of all the things said to me as a child: "How could you do that? Why would you make such a dumb decision? I can't believe you!" When I made a mistake as a child, I would be condemned without anyone ever telling me it was ok to make a mistake. That things happen. That the best way for me to grow and learn is to make mistakes. So, I spent a good portion of my life never understanding that mistakes can be good as long as you learn from them and change your approach next time. I told myself that if I wasn't perfect, I wasn't worthy of receiving love, and didn't deserve to be successful. I let those thoughts continue to replay in my mind and tell me that I was unworthy of progressing forward and this prevented me from healing. What I didn't realize was that in order for me to move past the things of my past, I had to understand that God had already forgiven me. I had to come to terms with the fact that YES, I made decisions that took me down a very different path than other people, but without making those decisions, I would not be the woman that I am today and God is not through with me yet.

This was an eye-opener for me because I spent the majority of my life carrying this heavy weight of unforgiveness with me everywhere. It was like a huge rock that was attached to my foot with a chain. I had grown so accustomed to carrying it that I no longer noticed it was there. But, it constantly slowed me down. I would get right to the peak of the mountaintop in an area in my life, then bam, I would find a way to mess it up and prevent my success. It wasn't because I didn't think I was capable of achieving that success or lacked the ability to get there. It was because I had told myself for the last thirty years of my life that I wasn't worthy of having that in my life and I believed it. Then, I made it my reality. I spent more time destroying my own success at work than enjoying the benefits of being successful. I remained in a negative state of mind and looked-for ways to create constant failure because then I would have something to complain about to those who would feel sorry for me in my situation. Do you see the constant battle I put myself through?

How many of us do this to ourselves without even realizing it? We spend a ton of our time working towards the things that create misery in our lives instead of working harder to have the things that bring us joy. Misery is not what God wants for us. He wants us to be people of joy so we can leave an impact. He wants us to focus on the things that grow us, not destroy us. God wants us to realize that he made the ultimate sacrifice on the cross because he loved us first, and we did not have to do anything to earn his love. This was challenging for me to comprehend.

I didn't love myself for years. I also believed that God did not love me. I hated the person I was because of the mistakes I had made, the mask I would wear, and the constant battle of working super hard to impress everyone that I would come across. It was exhausting and unfulfilling. I wanted to be the confident person I was great at pretending to be, but deep down inside, I was lonely and depressed. I was an expert at reminding myself about my imperfections, my flaws, and the things I didn't have that others did. I spent so much time comparing my life to other people and focusing on the things I lacked that I didn't know how to accept that God had already forgiven me for my mistakes and that I was just as loved as the people I spent my time comparing myself to. I didn't realize that it was possible to fall in love with yourself until I did it in my own life and I hope that if you come to a place in your own life where you experience similar feelings, that this will give you some ideas to try.

Loving yourself is a lot like dating. When the love is new and fresh, you are excited and eager to learn as much as you can about that person you are interested in. You may experience that warm and fuzzy feeling inside and you want to spend every waking moment with that person. Then, as time passes by, that new relationship seems less exciting. You get into a routine and you may not experience the same feelings that you did in the beginning. You become complacent and forget that you still have to work on your relationship, which can lead to that relationship ending or some temporary unhappiness in the relationship. The same is also true for loving yourself. It requires work. It requires effort. I personally believe that it is possible to fall in and out of love with yourself in different seasons of your life, as I have been through this personally. Overtime, I began to notice that the seasons I was falling out of love with myself were also the times that I had put forth the least amount of effort towards doing the things that helped me continue to love myself. What I failed to realize was that in order to love myself, I have to work towards the things that help me love myself, constantly. There is not a one-time fix and love-myself=forever solution. It's just like learning a new language. It takes lots of practice to get better and even when you feel like you have it mastered, you still continue to learn new slang words, phrases, or trends that never existed in the beginning and it is constantly evolving. Seeing a biblical counselor helped me realize that there were a few steps that I had to take to begin loving myself again.

Step 1: In order for me to love myself, I had to first realize that God loves me and that I am worthy of receiving his love. When I made mistakes growing up, I let the hurtful words that were said to me define the level of love I was worthy of receiving. I would hear things like, "How could you make such a dumb decision?" and let them replay in my head over and over. Overtime, I had heard those hurtful words so much that I began to tell them to myself when I would make a mistake. I let that create a wall between myself and anyone who tried to show me love. I associated love with pain since I didn't have a true model of what love looked like growing up. I thought that you were supposed to have pain in a relationship to receive love. I became so dissatisfied with my own life that I would create misery in other people's lives to make me feel better. It would make me feel like I wasn't alone in my own misery since I didn't know how to deal with it at the time. Since these words were primarily spoken from my father, when I became a Christian I had a really hard time having a relationship with God. I associated my perception of how God loved me to what was modeled to me as a child from my father.

As a Christian, when I would make mistakes, I imagined God being so disappointed in me and looking for ways to curse me for sinning. The first bad thing that would happen to me after making a mistake, I would accept as God's little way of getting back at me. I accepted that I deserved that kind of treatment for my mistake, even if the bad thing that happened was in no way related to my mistake. Therefore, I did not have a desire to get into a closer relationship with God because I associated that with future pain. Having a biblical counselor helped me to see that the views I had of what God was like when I made mistakes was completely false. God died for my sins because his love for me was far greater than any father's love. His love was unconditional and he didn't love me less because I made a mistake. God loves me no matter what. Realizing that I had spent my entire life with a false perception of who I thought God was opened my heart to see God in a whole new light. I began to envision him as a heroic dad who comforted me during my times of struggles, held me accountable, and helped me through some tough times. While realizing this was a great first step, I still had some work to continue moving forward.

Step 2: I had to find ways to get to know God on a deeper level so I could feel comfortable having a relationship with him. I decided to start with a devotional, which I thought would be easy, but it wasn't at all. I had a hard time imagining what God's love looked like in real life. I couldn't perceive what kind of things he would say or do, how he would react when mistakes were made, or what his character looked like. I decided to try to find a good devotional that could help me learn more about God. I had a really hard time finding a devotional that I could connect with given my mental block from my false perception of what God was like. Most of the devotionals that I found did a great job of teaching what God was like, but I wanted to get to know God on a first-hand basis to feel comfortable learning more about him. I needed to hear words that depicted what God would be like if he were speaking to me directly. This was when my counselor suggested a devotional, *His Thoughts Toward Me* by Marie Chapian, to read. It even started some mornings saying things like 'my daughter,' and was written in a way that felt like God was talking directly to me. Overtime, it helped to redefine my perception of what God was like, the things he would say, and his never-ending love for me. It helped me begin to trust God and include him in my life more. This was another step closer to helping me love and forgive myself, but I still had to do one more thing.

Step 3: I had to ask God for forgiveness and put the past in the past. I spent so much of my life letting my past mistakes consume my present and future. I would constantly tear myself down, tell myself over and over what a huge screw up I was, and let that hold me back from doing great things with my life. The truth was that I never dealt with the initial problem. I had to come to terms with my past mistakes, forgive myself, and leave those mistakes where they belonged, in the past. Once I began my journey towards getting closer to God and working on loving myself, I was able to have enough courage to ask God for forgiveness and know that I received it. I knew that I had to learn to stop letting my past mistakes remain in my present and immediately thought of something that I could start doing to help me now.

When I was younger, I went to a church camp that taught us about forgiveness and letting go of your past. The camp counselors wanted us to go to the top of a mountain to a place where we could pray by ourselves and ask God for forgiveness for one thing we wanted to let go of, then we would write that thing on a rock and throw it off a cliff. Once it was thrown off that cliff, it was out of our lives. God had already forgiven us before we had that rock in our hands. He already knew what we were going to ask, for, but physically throwing that rock off that cliff with that thing in my life that I was looking to part with was a great representation of what God's forgiveness looks like in our lives. Once he forgives us, it is done. We don't have to ask God a million times to forgive us for the same thing. We just need to come to terms with the fact that God sacrificed his only son to forgive us in advance. We must realize that holding onto your past does not help you move towards a better future. God does not create us to be people of guilt. He creates us to turn our guilt into a testimony because guilt was never the intention, sharing your story was the intention and changing lives is the result. We will dig into this further in the last chapter.

Chapter 9

Are You Telling Your Story?

Have you ever heard a story that was so compelling, it inspired you to want to make a change in your own life? A story that was so powerful, you no longer felt alone in facing the things you were going through? A story where you were given a new light on how to face a situation that you never knew there was an explanation for in the first place? This is the power that your story can have on other people's lives if you would embrace it and share it. I spent years never understanding the power of sharing my own story, only to realize that my story was meant to do more than just be my story. It was meant to be the hope in other people's stories. It was meant to help others not feel so alone in the things they were facing. It was meant to inspire other people to make a change, to create a different ending to their own life. Your story has no impact if it is kept a secret. You can't use it to create change if you don't share it. Not sharing your story would be like having an incredible weight loss regiment that is proven to produce massive life changing results, yet never sharing it with the world. No one would benefit except you. That is not God's intention when he created us to live in this world. We are put on this earth to share the gospel, which can be shared through our personal testimony, in a way that leads people toward salvation, so that in the end, God will receive the glory. We continue to get better over time, so we can defy the odds. This was when it hit me. I had been achieving great success for years, but for the wrong reason. I let my personal pride hold me back from sharing my story with the world and I want to encourage you with this story to consider sharing your own story.

I was a single parent, a teenage mother, and a person who many assumed would be a high school dropout, who wouldn't go to college, and who would never be able to create wealth or success. But, I had a choice to make. I could follow the opinions of other people, validate that they were right all along, and become the failure that they all expected, or I could shock everyone to the point that they watch in awe and wonder how I came out on top. I had adversities in my life. I had setbacks. I didn't live a perfect life and most of that was created as a result of my decisions. I accept full responsibility for my actions. However, I decided that despite everything, I would not let that define me. I let that push me forward. I let that keep me going. I let that move me in a new direction. I wanted to prove to everyone who doubted me that just because you make mistakes, it does not have to slow you down. Mistakes do not define who you are as a person or the level of success that you will achieve. Mistakes are your greatest asset if you learn and grow from them. You are the deciding factor of how things turn out in your life, not everyone else. This was where it all started.

I spent the majority of my life proving to other people that I wasn't a failure. I graduated #10 in my high school graduating class with many honors awards. I was the first person in my family to graduate from college. I landed a position with a big well-known company that promoted based on performance. I was able to become a branch manager with this company in a little over a year, which was unheard of, and later land an even higher paying sales position with the same company only months later. I lived what others would perceive as a great life. I had it all. I became the success that everyone else thought was impossible, all while raising my son. My life was quite the inspiration to many who observed, but I didn't see it that way. While I had all of these accomplishments under my belt, I never felt that they were enough. I would accomplish great things, yet still be unhappy in the end. I was unfulfilled and I couldn't figure out why.

One day, I had an experience that would allow me to gain clarity towards my purpose. I faced quite a bit of rejection and ridicule as a young mother in high school and I let that be the reason I was motivated to do even greater things with my life. I had always felt like I had to prove the people who doubted me wrong and show them that they had no idea what to expect. I wanted them to see my life and success and how great I turned out. I wanted to give them something to talk about, to dream about, to be confused about, so they would have no doubt in their mind that they were wrong about everything. But, there was a problem with this method. I was achieving great things for everyone else and not myself. Truth be told, I didn't even know half of the people who doubted me by name, just by the rumors that were said about me. Yet, I let the words that other people said about me play over and over in my head and hold me back from stepping into my purpose. I was more focused on proving everyone else wrong that I lost touch to the impact that God wanted me to have on the world. I worked so incredibly hard to show and prove my worth to the world that I forgot that it was my job to make an impact in a very different way. But first it had to start with me.

I had to get reconnected with my purpose, my reason for doing what I do every single day, and my 'why'. I had spent so much of my life relying on the opinions of how other people wanted me to live that I didn't even know my purpose. When I would think about what my purpose was, I would catch myself immediately referring back to what I thought other people would want to be my purpose and what would stand out to the most amount of people. I wanted to impress people in the world more than let God use me in the world. I was more concerned with looking cool and fun than serving God. I wanted to fit in more than stand out and be different. I didn't want the responsibility of doing God's work, which seemed more like work than fun in my eyes at the time. I had to realize that if I wanted to really figure out my true 'why', I had to involve God. I had to get real with God. I had to ask God for his hand to help me discover my purpose. I had no choice. So that's what I did. I asked God to help me start to see what my purpose was on this earth, what I was good at, and what I needed to be doing more of to serve him. God has an interesting way of getting through to you, sometimes in the least expected way, but this day it was through a customer. While this customer may have had no idea that God was using them to get through to me, my meeting with this customer, whom we will call Mrs. Jones for the purpose of the story, would become something I would never forget. This lesson was important because it helped to renew my faith.

It started out as a long series of phone conversations with a customer I wasn't sure I would ever move forward with, as she had a hectic schedule and wasn't sure that we would be able to help her with financing options because of some concerns she had with her credit. I had been selling cars for a highly reputable company for almost five years by this point and was confident that we could help her based off of what she had told me. I dealt with customers who had credit challenges all the time, so this was definitely not my first rodeo. I assured Mrs. Jones that I would do everything in my power to help her, but that I would like the opportunity to sit down with her to meet so that we could pick out a car that would be the right fit for her, as she was unsure what she was looking for in the first place. After multiple attempts of reaching out and phone conversations that went nowhere, I was ready to throw in the towel. I picked up the phone to dial her number with the intention of giving her the option of seeing if I could actually help or if I needed to remove her from my contact list. But, this time, my phone conversation with Mrs. Jones was very different. She picked up the phone and stated that she was actually on her way to come see me. She had just found out that she would be off work that evening and thanked me for my persistence and not giving up on her. Little did she know that I was actually calling her to do exactly that, had I not gotten anywhere with her. I made sure she had good directions to come see me and put her down for the time she had stated.

Once she arrived, I could tell from her nervous body language and lack of eye contact that she must have immediately regretted coming out to see me, that she was embarrassed of her credit situation, that she didn't really know why she came out, and that she lacked confidence in my ability to help her. I have always found it helpful to put customers at ease if I am at ease and if I look them in the eye and promise to do everything in my power to help them. I assured her that I was here to help and said a joke to get her laughing to ease the tension. She brought her husband with her. Together they seemed very defeated. It was hard to tell what was really going on in their lives, but I knew it was my job to eliminate the stress of car buying and help them narrow down a car that would best fit their budget and their needs. So, I proceeded to get to know them a little better so I could best understand what they would like to have in a vehicle and how I could help them.

Through getting to know Mr. and Mrs. Jones, I discovered that Mrs. Jones had had some prior health issues that got them into a financial bind, but she survived and immediately brought up how without God, she would not be here today. While she continued on and on about the struggles they had faced with her health, she always remained faithful to trusting God. She lit up when she spoke about God's healing in her life. It was apparent that she was a strong believer in God and that she trusted him with her health, but was obviously having some issues trusting him with helping her find the right vehicle and the right dealership to do business with. That made me really curious.

So, I began to ask her how car shopping had been going for her so far. Her entire countenance changed. A look of discouragement began to take over her face, and the joyful smile she had when she walked in began to disappear and it looked like tears were starting to form in her eyes. She proceeded to tell me that she had been to multiple dealerships and once she explained her situation to them, they would not give her the time of day. Without trying at all, they would explain that they did not think they were going to be able to help and left her with more anxiety than when she initially came in. After being told 'no' by so many people, it became very obvious to me that Mr. and Mrs. Jones stopped listening to God's voice in this area of their lives. I believe that they began to lose touch with the voice of God. They let the voices in the world tell them what was not possible for them and didn't listen to the one voice that mattered the most. They had stopped listening to God and began to believe what other people in the world said they could and could not do. That is when I realized that I could be the new voice for them. The voice that led them back to the faith they had deep down inside, but had let get buried below the surface of the negative voices from other people. They were at the end of their rope. They needed a glimpse of hope. They needed someone to believe in them and guide them towards the things that were possible for them. While God wants to be our first pick for situations like this, sometimes he uses other people to show you what is possible. That day, it was me.

We started by looking at a vehicle that I picked out for them based on what we discussed they were looking for. I pulled the vehicle up front and Mrs. Jones shrilled with excitement, as this had been her dream car for years but she never thought it would be possible to own one in her lifetime. We went on a test drive and she was in love. She was tired of owning super old vehicles that would break down all the time and marveled at how nice it would be to have a certified vehicle with a warranty and worry-free ownership. As we pulled into the dealership after finishing our test drive, I could see that same look of doubt take over her face. She began to see what the world had told her was impossible. I said, "Mrs. Jones, if this is the car that God wants you to have, he will open the doors and make it possible. If it is not, we will find something else. Will you have faith right now?" She agreed to have faith and watch God do the impossible. After several attempts, God made a way. We had one bank call us and let us know they would help her with financing. I refused to give up on her and we persisted until we found a way. As soon as we told her the news, she immediately went outside and raised both hands towards the sky and shouted, "Thank You God!" Mrs. Jones left in her dream car that day with tears in her eyes. She came in with no hope, defeated, and filled with doubt. She left a woman restored in her faith. Helping Mrs. Jones that day showed me that I have a much bigger purpose on this earth. I don't sell cars, I change lives one car at a time. I have the opportunity each day to either focus on hitting my goal or to focus on serving God. I have come to find that when you go in the direction that God wants for your life, you prosper far greater than you ever could on your own. I believe that at the end of our rope, when we are ready to give up, is where God is waiting for us. He is like the super strong brawny man waiting to take on the extra weight that we can't carry. He knows our limits. He knows when the weight is too much to carry. He challenges us, but he is always right there to pick up the weight we can't carry on our own. That is exactly where God stepped in for my customer that day, at the end of her tunnel, where she had no hope or certainty, and used me as a vessel to provide that for her in a time in my life where I felt that I had no purpose. Mr. and Mrs. Jones showed me my purpose that day and I will never forget it. Through learning about my purpose, I was more willing to begin using it to change lives by sharing my story.

It is harder for your story to leave a lasting impact when you are not willing to share the things you have experienced. God gives each and every one of us unique experiences to encounter so that we can share them with the world. We spend more time comparing our lives to other people and thinking of ways that we can portray our lives to be even better that we don't truly live our lives. We add filters to our Facebook photos, spend hours taking the same picture until it looks like it should belong in a magazine, and have pictures of our kids who are never messy and always wearing the perfect outfit for every picture. It is time to let people see the real you. It's time to give yourself permission to be transparent. It's time to start sharing your story.

Sharing your story will not only help you in dealing with your past, but it will help other people deal with their future. At a time where suicide rates are high, depression continues to rise, and anxiety is prevalent, you are helping create a positive trend that our society desperately needs. I believe that these illnesses occur in more individuals because we don't know how to deal with the root cause of our problems. We think that we can solve our own problems and therefore do not reach out to people for help. We're almost afraid to tell people that we have a problem because people in our society do a great job of pretending that they live a perfect life that we feel like the last man standing when we are presented with a problem in our own lives. We isolate ourselves and let the enemy continue to let us believe that we are not worthy of having a life of prosperity. Then, we medicate our problems that don't need medication. They need God. They need a consoler. They need stories, just like yours and mine, that are transparent and honest. They need to know that they are not alone in the problems they are facing. They need to know that someone else has already faced a similar problem and rose above it. They need to know that there is a way out.

They need your story. You never know whose life you are impacting from sharing your story. You never know who may be on the verge of giving up in their own life, but by hearing your story, may change the entire direction of their life. It's not up to you to worry about finding the people that you will impact, God will help with getting the right people in your presence. It is up to you to begin sharing your story because by sharing your story, you have the power to change the world.

Are You Telling Your Story?

Chapter 10

Telling My Story

"Your story is so much more than yourself, and God has created each and every one of us with a unique story that is made to be shared with the world."

I remember being a single mom in church looking at all of the other married couples and dreaming about how I wanted to be married one day so I wouldn't have to explain being a single parent to anyone else. I was tired of feeling like I had to prove and explain myself to other people. If I was married, I wouldn't have to explain why I didn't look old enough to have a kid, why I was a single parent, or how old I was when I had my son, because I was married and that all goes away, right? WRONG. It was when I got married that God began doing his work in me to give me the courage that I needed to begin to tell my story.

I'm not going to lie and say that telling my story was easy and I was thrilled to do it. I knew that this would be an imperative part of my journey to help me heal from my personal struggles. I waited until I was almost 30 years old before I actually began to tell my story in church. I was embarrassed, ashamed, and didn't feel qualified to share my story. I didn't want to feel the shame of judging eyes gazing upon me. I didn't want to go to that dark place in my mind and let satan tell me all of the reasons why sharing my story was something I shouldn't do. But God kept pushing me to share it, and one day, I decided to listen.

I prayed and asked God to give me the courage to share my story. I was terrified. I wasn't ready to step up. I didn't think I had what it took to share a story in a compelling way that would change people's lives. This was when God decided to use someone who he knew would encourage me to take the next step.

At this stage in my life, Jeremy and I were engaged and going through pre-marriage counseling with our pastor. He was on the mission trip where we met and we were so excited to have the honor of having him marry us and be a part of our journey from the beginning. It was in this meeting that I began to share with him how I was struggling with my career and had begun asking God multiple times per day to take me beyond the limits that I have put on myself. I told him that I knew God had more for me, I just couldn't see it, so I asked him to help me see further. I told him how I put limits on myself, what I was capable of doing, and that I had asked God to show me that I am capable of doing so much more with God's help. After sharing this story, I realized that this encouraged my pastor to ask God to take him beyond limits that he had put on himself in his own life. He instantly replied, "You need to write a book about this because it could have such an impact on so many people's lives." It never crossed my mind to do something like write a book until that moment. God put the right person in my path at the right time who made me realize that this book is so much bigger than myself. This book is about changing lives by sharing my story. This book is about God using me to make a difference. I began to pray about it and ask God to bring me the right connections to make this dream a reality. I began to pray for strength and courage to feel comfortable enough to share my story, as I was still a little reluctant. It was when I began to rely on the strength of God to push me through my fears that it all changed for me.

I was at a women's conference with our church for the weekend. I love going to these conferences to gain a fresh perspective and a new light and to socialize and get to know people on a deeper level. At previous conferences, I was usually quiet as I would take in what I was learning and had no plans of letting people get to know me on a deeper level. I would listen and admire the courage that the other women had to share their story, but I never volunteered to share my own story. I thought my story was way worse than the things these women had to struggle with and it wasn't accepted from God as something that was spoken about in church. Little did I know, this would be a start toward my journey of healing.

This particular conference had smaller tables with less women sitting at them, which allowed for everyone to speak when it was time to discuss what we just learned. They had questions prepared and we would each draw a card randomly and answer accordingly. I drew my card and was presented to answer this question: "What impossible thing do you need to believe God for right now?" I knew in my heart that the impossible thing I needed to believe in God for that day was the courage to talk about my story for the first time in church. This opened up the gates for me to talk about the struggles of being not only a teen mom, but a single parent seeking God and a better path for me and my son. I told the ladies at my table my story. I spoke about my struggles in having a relationship with God. I spoke about not feeling worthy of God's love. I cried. I could barely talk without getting emotional, but something very different happened to me that day. The ladies at my table showed me a compassion, support, and an acceptance that I had never experienced before that day. Most importantly, it was as if the heavy weight that I let hold me down for so many years had been lifted off me and I experienced forgiveness from God for the first time in my life. While God had always forgiven me from the beginning, I didn't know what that really looked like until that day. I truly believe that God used the ladies at my table as a vessel to show me that my story mattered, that God wasn't giving up on me, and neither should I. So, this leads me to my next question, are you telling your story?

I used to think that I had to wait until everything in my life was perfect and that I had to have all of the answers before I could talk about the struggles I faced, but then I realized that was not true at all. You don't have to wait until you have it all figured out, you just need to begin sharing your story and let God figure it out. He will do his work through you in more ways than you could imagine. In the process of telling your story, God will help you heal while you are healing others. You will be making a difference in people's lives while God makes a difference in your life. God will help you come to peace with your brokenness and use it to change other people's lives while simultaneously changing YOUR life. Do you see God's motive here? He never gives up on helping YOU. He doesn't forget about YOU in your journey of healing. YOU benefit in the process while offering others hope for a new beginning in their own life.

God works in miraculous ways and has an excellent way of making sure everyone benefits in the process, without excluding the most important piece to his puzzle, YOU. If there is so much in it for you, what's stopping you from sharing your story? Fear, doubt, other people, satan, whatever your reason, remember that for every time you let a negative thought or a doubt hold you back, you are missing out on the opportunity to contribute positively to someone else's life OR to see the contribution from others in your own life. You should NEVER let a negative thought or doubt hold you back from changing someone's life or missing out on that change in your own life. Ever.

Now, some of you may be thinking this sounds great and all, but how do I start? Well, I'm so glad you asked.

I started by doing something I was afraid of and telling people my story who didn't know me on a deeper level. I made sure they were the right people that could encourage me and lift me up. By sharing my story, I was able to give others encouragement, who I didn't know faced similar challenges to mine. I also realized that I was not alone in my journey. That encouragement gave me the courage to share my story again and again and eventually write this book. You start by taking a step towards the one thing that scares you the most. You do that one thing that scares you over and over until it no longer scares you anymore. That is how you build courage. God does not create us to be people of fear. "For God has not given us a spirit of fear and timidity, but of power, love, and self-discipline." (2 Timothy 1:7) He creates us to be people with audacity so great that the enemy has no choice but to fold.

It was in my place of loneliness that I let satan put thoughts in my head that I wasn't worthy, qualified, or capable of sharing my story in a way that would inspire and encourage other people. I secluded myself from the world by not telling my story and I let satan make me believe that staying complacent was better than running towards the things that were scary, even if God was right beside me. I failed to recognize the very truth in Exodus 14:14 that says, "The Lord himself will fight for you. Just stay calm." I let the thoughts that I wasn't worthy to share my story consume me so much that I didn't take action towards the things God needed me to in order to help me grow. Therefore, I was much like a stationary bike; the wheels keep spinning over and over, yet the bike never progresses in a forward direction. It was when I finally decided to move and take action to face my greatest fear by sharing my story that I began to experience healing. This was what I needed for the mistakes I made in my past to be able to walk with God towards the things I needed to accomplish in my future. While sharing my story was the beginning of my own healing, now it is the beginning of other people's healing.

My journey to learning how to look beyond the pain of my past ended up being someone else's journey to give them hope of a better future. Your story is unique and something you should be proud of, no matter what imperfections have happened in your life. Your story is so much more than yourself, and God has created each and every one of us with a unique story that is made to be shared with the world. I ran away from God for the first part of my life. I still run from God every now and then. We all do. What I have found is that in those moments of running, God finds a way to make his presence known. It was when I ran from God that I became closer to God, because for the first time in my life, I realized that through all the mistakes I made, through all the times I didn't see God's plan for my life, he never stopped loving me. He never stopped working to help me. He never gave up on me. He never stopped being my Savior. God gives us all the signs along the way. It's up to us to see the signs and follow his ways. We always have the choice.

If we decide to go the other way, God will still fulfil his promises, we just may not be involved in that particular part of his story. But, if we decide to follow God's path, he will take us down a back road that we never knew existed. He will show us things that we never knew were possible. He will help us see further. He will help us go further. He will help us go beyond any limits that we have put on ourselves. We cannot do this alone and we cannot do this without God. I believe that we go in and out of God's story in different parts of our life. This is what makes us unique. It's what makes our stories our own. It is what separates us from the rest of the world. We have different experiences that we go through so that we can now go into the world and share them with other people. In Matthew 5:14-16, God says, "You are the light of the world – like a city on a hilltop that cannot be hidden. No one lights a lamp and then puts it under the basket. Instead, a lamp is placed on a stand, where it gives light to everyone in the house. In the same way, let your good deeds shine out for all to see, so that everyone will praise your heavenly father." It is up to us to either keep our stories the same or let God take our stories to the next level. It is up to us to share our 'beyond limits' story. We all have the capability. We all have the power. We all have the skill. My story would not be possible had I not made the decision to seek God first, follow his ways and not my own, and trust his plan for my life.

My 'beyond limits' story involves a single, teen mother trying to find herself. In her search, she found a God who helped her begin to love herself again.

She found a God who loves her unconditionally, she attracted a man who would love her exactly how God knew she needed to be loved, because he hand picked him for her. He was just waiting for the right moment to bring them together. This man would become her loving husband, Jeremy, a short time later. Her son, Landon, turned out to be an inspiration to everyone who knows him. He is confident, smart, and has an incredible blended family who supports him in everything he does. None of this would be possible without God and none of this would be known without sharing my story.

Who are you going to begin sharing your story with today?

Telling My Story

"It's funny how God works in our lives when we trust in him.

He gives us everything we could have ever wanted and more.

We have the choice to trust.

We have the choice to follow.

We have the choice to go.

God always leaves the choice to us.

What will YOU Choose?"

- Kelli Boone

BEYOND LIMITS

About the Author

As a mom, business woman, wife, and runner, who somehow finds time to write books on the side, Kelli specializes in helping people change their perception of themselves and their capabilities by showing them simple strategies they can use in their personal lives every day. With her fire for God, her passion for learning, and her neuroscience background, she is obsessed with teaching people how to change their thought patterns to shift the direction of their life. She has an energy that will fill a room and is ready to help you take your life to the next level.

www.KelliBoone.com

BEYOND LIMITS

BEYOND LIMITS

Disclaimer & Copyright Information

Some of the events, locales, and conversations have been recreated from memories. In order to maintain their anonymity, in some instances, the names of individuals and places have been changed. As such, some identifying characteristics and details may have changed.

Although the author and publisher have made every effort to ensure that the information in this book was correct at press time, the author and publisher do not assume and hereby disclaim any liability to any party for any loss, damage, or disruption caused by errors or omissions, whether such errors or omissions result from negligence, accident, or any other cause.

All quotes, unless otherwise noted,
are attributed to the respective author or to the Holy Bible.

Cover illustration, book design and production
Copyright © 2017 by Tribute Publishing, LLC
www.TributePublishing.com

Scripture references are copyrighted by www.BibleGateway.com which is operated by the Zondervan Corporation, L.L.C

BEYOND LIMITS

BEYOND LIMITS

www.ingramcontent.com/pod-product-compliance
Lightning Source LLC
Chambersburg PA
CBHW021130300426
44113CB00006B/371